ENGLISH - THAI

Pocket Book

D0324757

All you have to know !

ENGLISH - THAI

Pocket book, 2nd edition 2002

Text by

Georg Gensbichler

Sarika Puangsombat

Illustrations by

BanDon

ISBN 974-272-143-2

Published by

HOT & SPICY CO., LTD.

Copyright©   HOT & SPICY CO., LTD.
                Fax Thailand: (66) - 2 - 914 1425
                Fax USA: (1) - 209 - 671 7536
                E-mail: mail@hotspicy.co.th
                Internet: http://www.hotspicy.co.th

Printed in Thailand

The publishers wish to thank **Mr. Sylvester van Welij** for all his effort and help in making this revised edition possible.

ENGLISH - THAI

All you have to know !

Contents

CONTENTS

CONTENTS

CONTENTS

Need to know more ?

The fun way to learn the language !

THAI   LANGUAGE

Introduction

This extended version of our popular **"English - Thai - Holidays Language - Guide"** *covers a wider range of the Thai language and should be helpful for the tourist as also for the foreigner living in Thailand. One should be able to understand the most important phrases and have some small talk with the Thai people. We hope you enjoy learning the Thai language and wish you all the best.*
But it is very important to learn the correct pronunciation and use of tones from a Thai, otherwise you won't be understood.

Correct pronunciation of the different tones:

The different tones:

Each Thai word can have 5 different meanings if different tones are used.
But note: not all words use all 5 tones.

Introduction to the 5 different tones:

1. middle tone:

without symbol   common tone, pronounced flat
all syllables without symbol should
be pronounced flat in this book

e.g.: **maa** = come

มา

2. low tone:

symbol: ↓   similar to middle tone
voice drops lower than normal

↓
e.g.: **mai** = new   ใหม่

3. falling tone:

symbol: ก   pronounced falling
like an emphatic pronunciation in
English

ก
e.g.: **mai** = not   ไม่

4. high tone:

symbol: usually the most difficult.
                   voice goes up higher than normal

                         e.g.: **maa = horse**   ม้า

5. rising tone:

symbol: like the English question tone

                         e.g.: **maa = dog**   หมา

Polite   syllables

Whenever you speak Thai you should use the syllable
***'khrap'** or **'kha'** at the end of the sentence.*
*If you are male you use **'khrap'** and if you are female*
*you use **'kha'** at the end of each sentence.*

The Thai alphabet

Following a list of all consonants and vowels of the Thai alphabet.

consonant	initial	final	closest English	note
ป	p	p	spit	not aspirated
ต ฏ	t	t	step	not aspirated
ก	k	k	skin	not aspirated
พ ภ ผ	ph	p	pen	aspirated p, never as: phone
ท ธ ฒ ฑ ถ ฐ	th	t	tea	aspirated t, never as: the
ค ฆ ข	kh	k	king	aspirated k
บ	b	p	bed	
ด ฎ	d	t	dock	
จ	j	t	jet	omit the z sound inside it
ม	m	m	man	
น ณ	n	n	nine	
ง	ng	ng	sing	can also occur at begin
ฟ ฝ	f	p	fit	
ส ศ ษ ซ	s	t	sit	
ห ฮ	h		hall	

consonant	initial	final	closest English	note
ฉ ช ฌ	ch	t	check	
ร	r	n	room	
ล ฬ	l	n	lock	
ว	w	w	wing	
ย ญ	y	i	young	
อ	-	- (silent)		used if begins with vowel sound

ก ข ฃ ค ฅ ฆ ง จ ฉ ช ซ ฌ ญ ฎ ฏ ฐ
ฑ ฒ ณ ด ต ถ ท ธ น บ ป ผ ฝ พ ฟ
ภ ม ย ร ล ว ศ ษ ส ห ฬ อ ฮ

–ะ –า –ิ –ี –ึ –ื –ุ –ู เ–ะ เ
แ–ะ แ– โ–ะ โ– เ–าะ อ –ัวะ –ัว
เ–ียะ เ–ีย เ–ือะ เ–ือ เ–อะ เ–อ –ำ
ใ– ไ– เ–า ฤ ฤๅ ฦ ฦๅ

The vowels can be positioned before, after, above or under the consonants.

long vowel	phonetic	English	Thai word	meaning
-า	aa	plaza	plaa	fish
เ	e	plain	khet	zone
แ	ae	pan	mae	mother
̅	ee	green	mee	have
โ	oh	home	lohk	world
-อ	aw	lawn	hawng	room
ุ̅	uu	moon	muu	pork
̅ือ ̅ื	ue	lure	mue	hand
เ-อ เ ̅อ	oe	fur	doen	walk
ไ ใ	ai	dye	mai	not
-าว	aao	brow	khaao	rice
̅ัว - ว	ua	poor	wua	cow
เ ̅ือ	uea	pure	kluea	salt
เ ̅ีย	ia	beer	mia	wife
เ ̅ียว	io	new	khio	green
เ ̅ือย	uei		nuei	tired
เ-ย	oei		khoei	ever

15

short vowel		phonetic		English	Thai word	meaning
–ะ	–ั	a'	a	far	rak	love
เ–ะ	เ–็	e'	e	let	lek	small
แ–ะ	แ–็	ae'	ae	mat	lae'	and
–ิ	–ิ	i'	i	feet	khit	think
โ–ะ		o'	o	boat	phop	meet
เ–าะ		o'		lot	ko'	island
–ุ	–ุ	u'	u	book	thuk	every
–ึ	–ึ	ue'	ue	luck[1]	khuen	rise
เ–อะ		oe'		hut[2]	yoe'	many
–ัย		ai				
เ–า		ao		loud	bao	light
–ัวะ		ua'				
เ–ือะ		uea'				
เ–ียะ		ia'			pawpia'	spring roll
–ำ		am		farm	nam	water

Notes:

[1] like in French "tu" or German "Umlaut - u (ü)"

[2] not too far from the English hut (think of "Pizza hut"). Another example could be the golf term "putt", or the more familiar "nut"

16

Log on to **www.hotspicy.co.th** and see a full list of available titles.

Online ordering available - we deliver worldwide!

Golf Resorts of Thailand

Where to play & stay

www.golfasian.com

17

GREETINGS

Good Morning !		
Good Afternoon !	Sawatdee khrap (kha) !	
Good Evening !	สวัสดี ครับ (ค่ะ)	
I (male)	**phom**	**ผม**
I (female)	**dee chan, chan**	**ดิฉัน,ฉัน**
you	khun	คุณ
he, she	khao	เขา
it	man	มัน
we	(phuak)rao	พวกเรา
you	(phuak)khun	พวกคุณ
they	(phuak)khao	พวกเขา
mine, my	khawng phom	ของผม
mine, my	khawng chan	ของฉัน
yours	khawng khun	ของคุณ
his, her	khawng khao	ของเขา
our	khawng phuakrao	ของพวกเรา
yours	khawng phuakkhun	ของพวกคุณ
theirs	khawng phuakkhao	ของพวกเขา

19

First examples...

Welcome to Thailand

Yindee tawn rap !
ยินดีต้อนรับ

How are you ?

Sabaai dee mai khrap ?
สบายดีไหมครับ

Thanks, fine.

Sabaai dee khrap.
สบายดีครับ

What is your name ?

Khun chue arai khrap ?
คุณชื่ออะไรครับ

My name is...

Phom chue...
ผมชื่อ...

I am glad to meet you.

Phom dee jai tee dai phop khun.
ผมดีใจที่ได้พบคุณ

Thank you.

Khawp khun khrap.
ขอบคุณครับ

I don't understand.

Phom mai khao jai.

ผมไม่เข้าใจ

Please speak more slowly !

Chuai phuut chaa chaa noi !

ช่วยพูดช้าๆหน่อย

Please speak louder !

Chuai phuut dang dang noi !

ช่วยพูดดังๆหน่อย

Please say again !

Chuai phuut eek khrang !

ช่วยพูดอีกครั้ง

How do you call this in Thai ?

Nee phaasaa Thai riak waa arai ?

นี่ภาษาไทยเรียกว่าอะไร

Do I pronounce it correctly ?

Phom awk siang thuuk mai khrap ?

ผมออกเสียงถูกไหมครับ

Bye bye.

Laa gawn.

ลาก่อน

See you later.

Laeo phop kan na'.

แล้วพบกันนะ

See you tomorrow.

Phrung nee phop kan.

พรุ่งนี้พบกัน

See you soon.

Laeo phop kan mai.

แล้วพบกันใหม่

Good luck.

Chohk dee na' !

โชคดีนะ

My regards to...

Faak khwaam khit thueng...

ฝากความคิดถึง...

VERBS

What you always hear...

English	Transliteration	Thai
ask	thăam	ถาม
be	pen	เป็น
be (located)	yùu	อยู่
buy	súe	ซื้อ
can, be able	dâi	ได้
carry *things*	thŭe	ถือ
carry *persons*	ûm	อุ้ม
come	maa	มา
do, make	tham	ทำ
drink	dùem	ดื่ม
eat	kin (thaan) khâao	กินข้าว,ทานข้าว
find	phóp	พบ
forget	luem	ลืม
give	hâi	ให้
go	pai	ไป
go out	pai thîo	ไปเที่ยว
have	mee	มี
hear	dâi yin	ได้ยิน

25

VERBS

help	chuai	ช่วย
know	ruu jak	รู้จัก
laugh	hua ro'	หัวเราะ
like	chawp	ชอบ
live, reside	yuu	อยู่
look	duu, mawng	ดู, มอง
look for, search	haa	หา
love	rak	รัก
must	tawng	ต้อง
need, want	tawng kaan	ต้องการ
pay	jaai ngoen	จ่ายเงิน
play	len	เล่น
read	aan	อ่าน
remember	jam	จำ
see	hen	เห็น
sell	khaai	ขาย
sit	nang	นั่ง
sleep	nawn	นอน
smile	yim	ยิ้ม

26

speak	phuut	พูด
swim	waai nam	ว่ายน้ำ
take	ao	เอา
tell	bawk	บอก
understand	khao jai	เข้าใจ
wait	raw	รอ
want	yaak	อยาก
wash, launder	sak	ซัก
wash, shampoo	sa	สระ
wash, clean	laang	ล้าง
work	tham ngaan	ทำงาน
write	khian	เขียน

sak phaa = wash clothes   ซักผ้า
sa' phom = shampoo one's hair สระผม
laang mue = wash one's hands ล้างมือ

A d d i t i o n a l   v e r b s

AAA

accompany	song	ส่ง
add up	buak	บวก
advertise	tham khohsanaa	ทำโฆษณา
agree	hen duai	เห็นด้วย
announce	pra'kaat	ประกาศ
answer	toop	ตอบ
arrive	maa thueng	มาถึง
assist, help	chuai luea	ช่วยเหลือ
assume	sommat	สมมติ
attack	johm tee	โจมตี

BBB

begin, start	roem	เริ่ม
believe	chuea	เชื่อ
bet	phanan	พนัน
blossom	baan	บาน
borrow	khaw yuem	ขอยืม
break	hak	หัก

| build | saang | สร้าง |

CCC

call (phone)	thoh pai haa	โทรไปหา
cancel	yok loek	ยกเลิก
celebrate	chalawng	ฉลอง
change	plian	เปลี่ยน
chase away	lai, lai pai	ไล่, ไล่ไป
check, examine	truat	ตรวจ
climb	peen	ปีน
close	pit	ปิด
collect	sa'som	สะสม
command	sang	สั่ง
complain	bon	บ่น
convince	tham hai chuea man	ทำให้เชื่อมั่น
cook	tham kap khaao	ทำกับข้าว
correct	kaekhai	แก้ไข
count	nap lek	นับเลข
cry	rawng hai	ร้องให้
cut	tat	ตัด

DDD

English	Transliteration	Thai
dance	tenram	เต้นรำ
deliver	faak	ฝาก
deliver	song hai	ส่งให้
dig	kut	ขุด
discover	khon phop	ค้นพบ
divide	haan	หาร
dream	fan	ฝัน
dust	pat fun	ปัดฝุ่น

EEE

English	Transliteration	Thai
end, finish	loek	เลิก
escape, flee	nee	หนี
explain	athibaai	อธิบาย
export	song awk	ส่งออก

FFF

English	Transliteration	Thai
feed	hai aahaan	ให้อาหาร
feel	ruusuek	รู้สึก
find	phop	พบ

flirt	láo lohm	เล้าโลม
follow	tit taam	ติดตาม
forecast, predict	tham naai	ทำนาย
fry	thâwt	ทอด

GGG

gain (weight)	phôem nám nàk	เพิ่มน้ำหนัก
gather, assemble	rûam kan	ร่วมกัน
get up	tùen	ตื่น
give	yók hâi	ยกให้
go down(stairs)	long bandai	ลงบันได
go for a walk	doen len	เดินเล่น
go up(stairs)	khûen bandai	ขึ้นบันได
grow	plùuk	ปลูก

HHH

hang	khwǎen	แขวน
happen	kòet	เกิด
hate	klìat	เกลียด
hide	sâwn	ซ่อน
hit	tee	ตี

hope	wǎng	หวัง
hunt	lâa	ล่า

I I I, JJJ

ice-skate	lên sakét	เล่นสเก็ต
import	nam khâo	นำเข้า
interrupt	khàt jang wà'	ขัดจังหวะ
invent	pradìt	ประดิษฐ์
invite	chuan	ชวน
joke	phûut talòk	พูดตลก
jump	kra'dòht	กระโดด

KKK

kick	tè'	เตะ
kiss	hǎwm	หอม
kiss (on the cheeks)	jùup	จูบ
knock (ring the bell)	kòt kradìng	กดกระดิ่ง
knock (on the door)	khó' pra'tuu	เคาะประตู

LLL

leave, abandon	àwk jàak	ออกจาก

lend	haî yuem	ให้ยืม
let, lease, rent out	haî chaô	ให้เช่า
lie	kohhok	โกหก
listen	fang	ฟัง
look after, take care	faô	เฝ้า
lose	phae	แพ้

MMM

manage	jat kaan	จัดการ
marry	taeng ngaan	แต่งงาน
misunderstand	khaô jai phit	เข้าใจผิด
mow	tat yaa	ตัดหญ้า
multiply	khoon	คูณ

NNN

need, require	jaai	จ่าย

OOO

open	poet	เปิด
order	sang	สั่ง

33

PPP

paint	thaa see	ทาสี
pay	kep ngoen	เก็บเงิน
persuade	chak chuan	ชักชวน
pick up, come for	rap	รับ
pick up, lift	yok, kep	ยก, เก็บ
plough, plow	thai naa	ไถนา
point to	chee	ชี้
pour	the	เท
prevent	pawng kan	ป้องกัน
produce	phalit	ผลิต
pull	dueng	ดึง
punch	toi	ต่อย
punish	long thoht	ลงโทษ
push	plak	ผลัก

QQQ

quarrel	tha'lo'	ทะเลาะ

RRR

receive	dai rap	ได้รับ
register	long thabian	ลงทะเบียน
remove,clear away	kep khong	เก็บของ
renew	taw aayu'	ต่ออายุ
rent, lease	chao	เช่า
repair	sawm	ซ่อม
respect	khaorop	เคารพ
rest	phak, phak nuei	พัก, พักเหนื่อย
run	wing	วิ่ง

SSS

send	song	ส่ง
shoot	ying	ยิง
shout	ta'kohn	ตะโกน
sing	rawng phleng	ร้องเพลง
slimming	lot nam nak	ลดน้ำหนัก
smell	domklin	ดมกลิ่น
smoke	suup buree	สูบบุหรี่
spell	sa'kot	สะกด

VERBS

stand	yuen	ยืน
start, begin	roem	เริ่ม
stitch, sew	yep	เย็บ
subtract	lop	ลบ
suggest	sanoe	เสนอ
suppose, guess	songsai	สงสัย

TTT

take a ride	khap rot len	ขับรถเล่น
taste	chim	ชิม
teach	sawn	สอน
think	khit	คิด
throw	paa, yohn	ปา, โยน
touch, grab	jap	จับ
translate	plae	แปล
travel	doenthaang	เดินทาง
try	phayaayaam	พยายาม
try, attempt	phayaayaam, lawng	พยายาม, ลอง

VVV

vaccuum, hoover	duut fun	ดูดฝุ่น
visit	pai hǎa, yiamyian	ไปหา, เยี่ยมเยียน

WWW

wake up	pluk	ปลุก
walk	doen	เดิน
waste	sia	เสีย
whisper	kra'sip	กระซิบ
win	chana'	ชนะ
wipe	chet	เช็ด
work on, deal with	triam	เตรียม

ADJECTIVES

big	yai	ใหญ่
small	**lek**	**เล็ก**
cheap	thuuk	ถูก
expensive	phaeng	แพง
clean	**sa aat**	**สะอาด**
dirty	**sokkaprok**	**สกปรก**
dangerous	antaraai	อันตราย
safe	plawt phai	ปลอดภัย
dark	**muet**	**มืด**
light	**sawaang**	**สว่าง**
easy	ngaai	ง่าย
difficult	yaak	ยาก
empty	**waang, plao**	**ว่าง, เปล่า**
full	**tem**	**เต็ม**
fat	uan	อ้วน
thin, slim	phawm	ผอม
thick	**naa**	**หนา**
thin	**baang**	**บาง**
good	dee	ดี
bad	leo	เลว

hard	khaeng	แข็ง
soft	num / awn	นุ่ม / อ่อน
hot	rawn	ร้อน
cold	naao / yen	หนาว/เย็น
illegal	phit kot maai	ผิดกฎหมาย
legal	thuuk kot maai	ถูกกฎหมาย
light	bao	เบา
heavy	nak	หนัก
little	noi	น้อย
a lot, plenty	maak	มาก
loud	dang	ดัง
quiet	bao	เบา
near	klai	ใกล้
far	klai	ไกล
old	kao	เก่า
new	mai	ใหม่
old	kae	แก่
young (girl)	saao	สาว
young (boy)	num	หนุ่ม

Be careful with the pronunciation!

English	Transliteration	Thai
ordinary	thammadaa	ธรรมดา
special	pheeset	พิเศษ
poor	**jon**	**จน**
rich	**ruai**	**รวย**
ripe	suk	สุก
unripe	dip	ดิบ
shallow	**tuen**	**ตื้น**
deep	**luek**	**ลึก**
short	san	สั้น
long	naan	นาน
short	**san**	**สั้น**
long	**yao**	**ยาว**
silly	ngoh	โง่
clever	chalaad	ฉลาด
skilful	**keng**	**เก่ง**
clumsy	**ngum ngaam**	**งุ่มง่าม**
slow	chaa	ช้า
quick	reo	เร็ว
tidy, neat	**riap roi**	**เรียบร้อย**
untidy	**loe' thoe'**	**เลอะเทอะ**

ADJECTIVES

English	Transliteration	Thai
ugly	kheere	ขี้เหร่
beautiful	suai	สวย
weak	**awn ae**	**อ่อนแอ**
strong	**khaeng raeng**	**แข็งแรง**
wide	kwaang	กว้าง
narrow	khaep	แคบ
wet	**piak**	**เปียก**
try	**haeng**	**แห้ง**
wrong	phit	ผิด
right	thuuk	ถูก

QUESTION and ANSWER

Questions words

> *There are two ways to form a question:*
> *1. use any of the listed question words*
> *or*
> *2. add the word '**mai**' at the end of the sentence*

How ?	yang ngai	ยังไง
How far ?	klai thaorai	ไกลเท่าไร
How many ?	kee	กี่
How much ?	thaorai	เท่าไร
What ?	arai	อะไร
When ?	mue-arai	เมื่อไร
Why ?	thammai	ทำไม
Where ?	theenai	ที่ไหน
Where from ?	jaak nai	จากไหน
Where to ?	(pai) nai	(ไป) ไหน
Which ?	(an) nai	(อัน) ไหน
Which way ?	thaang nai	ทางไหน
Who ?	khrai	ใคร
Who ?	(khon) nai	(คน) ไหน

When will you come back again ?

Khun ja' klap maa <u>mue-arai</u> ?
คุณจะกลับมาเมื่อไร

Why don't you have a girlfriend ?

<u>Thammai</u> khun mai mee faen ?
ทำไมคุณไม่มีแฟน

What do you work ?

Khun tham ngaan <u>arai</u> ?
คุณทำงานอะไร

Who (which person) can speak Thai ?

<u>Khon nai</u> phuut phaasaa thai dai ?
คนไหนพูดภาษาไทยได้

Who can speak Thai ?

<u>Khrai</u> phuut phaasaa thai dai ?
ใครพูดภาษาไทยได้

Which sunglasses do you like ?

Khun chawp waentaa an nai ?

คุณชอบแว่นตาอันไหน

How far is it to the market ?

Talaat klai thaorai jaak theenee ?

ตลาดไกลเท่าไรจากที่นี่

How do you do that ?

Nee tham yaang ngai ?

นี่ทำยังไง

How much is it ?

Raakhaa thaorai ?

ราคาเท่าไร

How many siblings do you have ?

Khun mee peenawng kee khon ?

คุณมีพี่น้องกี่คน

Where do you live ?

Khun phak yuu <u>theenai</u> ?

คุณพักอยู่ที่ไหน

Where do you come from ?

Khun maa <u>jaak nai</u> ?

คุณมาจากไหน

Where do you go?

Khun pai <u>nai</u> ?

คุณไปไหน

Which is the way to the market ?

<u>Thaang nai</u> pai talaat ?

ทางไหนไปตลาด

To form a question without question word, just add the word 'mai' to the end of the sentence.

Can you speak Thai ?

Khun phuut phaasaa thai dai mai ?

คุณพูดภาษาไทยได้ไหม

YES and NO

1) *There is no easy answer for **YES** or **NO** in the Thai language.*
   All depends on the asked question.

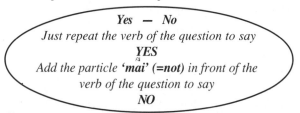

> **Yes — No**
> *Just repeat the verb of the question to say*
> **YES**
> *Add the particle **'mai'** (=**not**) in front of the verb of the question to say*
> **NO**

2) *Many times the question will end with the particle*
   '...chai mai' (= isn't it?)
   *The answer with **'chai'** means **YES** and*
   *'mai chai' means **NO**.*

yes	chai	ใช่
no	mai chai	ไม่ใช่

3) *You can also use the particle **'khrap'** or **'kha'** for*
   YES
   *and **'mai khrap'** or **'mai kha'** for **NO**.*

yes	khrap / kha	ครับ / ค่ะ
no	mai khrap /	ไม่ครับ /
	mai kha	ไม่ค่ะ

QUESTION & ANSWER

Additional words

question	kham thaam	คำถาม
answer	kham tawp	คำตอบ
already	laeo	แล้ว
also, too	duai	ด้วย
although	yaang rai ko dee	อย่างไรก็ดี
and, and then	lae', laeo ko	และ, แล้วก็
because	phro' waa	เพราะว่า
but	tae	แต่
if, when	thaa	ถ้า
in case of	phuea waa	เผื่อว่า
maybe, perhaps	aat ja'	อาจจะ
nevertheless	mae waa	แม้ว่า
only	thaonan	เท่านั้น
or	rue	หรือ
or not yet?	laeo rue yang	แล้วหรือยัง
possibly	khong ja'	คงจะ
with	kap	กับ
yet, not yet	yang, yang mai	ยัง, ยังไม่

You are in a hurry ?

All you need to know to keep going.

This little book will help you get by in Thailand !

NUMBERS and COUNTING

Numbers

๐	0	sǔun	ศูนย์
๑	1	nueng	หนึ่ง
๒	2	sǎwng	สอง
๓	3	sǎam	สาม
๔	4	see	สี่
๕	5	haa	ห้า
๖	6	hok	หก
๗	7	jet	เจ็ด
๘	8	paet	แปด
๙	9	gao	เก้า
๑๐	10	sip	สิบ
๑๑	11	sip-et	สิบเอ็ด
๑๒	12	sip-sǎwng	สิบสอง
๒๐	20	yee-sip	ยี่สิบ
๒๑	21	yee-sip-et	ยี่สิบเอ็ด
๓๐	30	sǎam-sip	สามสิบ
๑๐๐	100	nueng roi	หนึ่งร้อย
๓๒๕	325	sǎam roi yee-sip-haa	สามร้อยยี่สิบห้า

NUMBERS & COUNTING

๑๐๐๐	1.000	nueng phan	หนึ่งพัน
๑๐๐๐๐	10.000	nueng muen	หนึ่งหมื่น
๑๐๐๐๐๐	100.000	nueng saen	หนึ่งแสน
๑๐๐๐๐๐๐	1,000.000	nueng laan	หนึ่งล้าน

dozen	loh	โหล
pair	khuu	คู่
first time	khrang raek	ครั้งแรก
last time	khrang sut thaai	ครั้งสุดท้าย

Counting

2 children   luuk sawng khon ลูกสองคน
(child - 2 - classification)

3 cars   rot saam khan รถสามคัน
(car - 3 - classification)

*If you can't remember the correct particle,
you can use the word 'an'.*

Classification

To count things or people in the Thai language, you have to use special words, particles (classification). You just add this particle to the word.

> *There are about 80 different particles !*

particle for	particle	
cars	khan	คัน
trees	ton	ต้น
flowers, joss sticks	dawk	ดอก
letters, newspapers	chabap	ฉบับ
books, candles, knives	lem	เล่ม
elect. appliances (TV, radio)	khrueang	เครื่อง
fruits	luuk	ลูก
houses, closet, cupboard	lang	หลัง
dress, suit	chut	ชุด
small things	**an**	อัน
people	khon	คน
glasses, dishes, photos	bai	ใบ
animals, clothes, furniture	tua	ตัว

TIME & DATE

T i m e

'tee ': *night time*

0:00	thiang khuen	เที่ยงคืน
1:00	tee nueng	ตีหนึ่ง
2:00	tee sawng	ตีสอง
3:00	tee saam	ตีสาม
4:00	tee see	ตีสี่
5:00	tee haa	ตีห้า

'mohng chao': *morning*

6:00	hok mohng chao	หกโมงเช้า
7:00	nueng mohng chao	หนึ่งโมงเช้า
8:00	sawng mohng chao	สองโมงเช้า
9:00	saam mohng chao	สามโมงเช้า
10:00	see mohng chao	สี่โมงเช้า
11:00	haa mohng chao	ห้าโมงเช้า

57

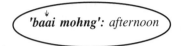

'baai mohng': *afternoon*

12:00	thi-ang wan	เที่ยงวัน
13:00	baai (nueng) mohng	บ่าย(หนึ่ง)โมง
14:00	baai sawng mohng	บ่ายสองโมง
15:00	baai saam mohng	บ่ายสามโมง
16:00	baai see mohng	บ่ายสี่โมง
17:00	baai haa mohng	บ่ายห้าโมง

'thum': *evening*

18:00	hok mohng yen	หกโมงเย็น
19:00	nueng thum	หนึ่งทุ่ม
20:00	sawng thum	สองทุ่ม
21:00	saam thum	สามทุ่ม
22:00	see thum	สี่ทุ่ม
23:00	haa thum	ห้าทุ่ม

| 14:30 | baai sǎwng mohng khrueng |
| | บ่ายสองโมงครึ่ง |

| 14.50 | eek sip naathee baai saam mohng |
| | อีกสิบนาทีบ่ายสามโมง |

> *Be careful:*
> *9 o'clock in the morning (= 3 mohng chao)*
> *3 o'clock in the afternoon (= baai 3 mohng)*
> *9 o'clock in the evening (= 3 thum)*

What is the time?	Kee mohng laeo	กี่โมงแล้ว
time	welaa	เวลา
hour	chua mohng	ชั่วโมง
half hour	khrueng chua mohng	ครึ่งชั่วโมง
minute	naathee	นาที
second	winaathee	วินาที
watch, clock	naalikaa	นาฬิกา

Date

Monday	wan jan	วันจันทร์
Tuesday	wan angkhaan	วันอังคาร
Wednesday	wan phut	วันพุธ
Thursday	wan pharuehat	วันพฤหัส
Friday	wan suk	วันศุกร์
Saturday	wan sao	วันเสาร์
Sunday	wan aathit	วันอาทิตย์

today	wan nee	วันนี้
yesterday	muea waan nee	เมื่อวานนี้
tomorrow	phrung nee	พรุ่งนี้
after tomorrow	ma'ruen nee	มะรืนนี้
before yesterday	muea waan suen	เมื่อวานซืน

morning	tawn chao	ตอนเช้า
afternoon	tawn baai	ตอนบ่าย
evening	tawn yen	ตอนเย็น
day / night	wan / khuen	วัน / คืน

| weekend | sao-aathit | เสาร์อาทิตย์ |
| week | aathit | อาทิตย์ |

Months

January	makaraa khom	มกราคม
February	kumphaa phan	กุมภาพันธ์
March	meenaa khom	มีนาคม
April	mesaa yon	เมษายน
May	phruetsaphaa khom	พฤษภาคม
June	mithunaa yon	มิถุนายน
July	karakadaa khom	กรกฎาคม
August	singhaa khom	สิงหาคม
September	kanyaa yon	กันยายน
October	tulaa khom	ตุลาคม
November	phruetsajikaa yon	พฤศจิกายน
December	thanwaa khom	ธันวาคม

month	duean	เดือน
beginning of month	ton duean	ต้นเดือน
end of month	plaai duean	ปลายเดือน

TIME & DATE

There are 3 seasons in Thailand:
1) **rueduu rawn:** *March - June*
2) **rueduu fon:** *July - October*
3) **rueduu naao:** *November - February*

season	rueduu	ฤดู
hot season	rueduu rawn	ฤดูร้อน
rainy season	rueduu fon	ฤดูฝน
cool season	rueduu naao	ฤดูหนาว
year	pee	ปี
century	satawat	ศตวรรษ
date	wan tee	วันที่

Date in Thai:
wan tee + number + month
for example : *August 16th =*
wan tee 16 (= sip hok) singhaa kho
วันที่ ๑๖ สิงหาคม

Additional words

after, when	lang jaak	หลังจาก
always	samoe, talawt pai	เสมอ, ตลอดไป
appointment, date	mee nat	มีนัด
approximate	pra'maan	ประมาณ
at, on	tee	ที่
before, ago	tee laeo	ที่แล้ว
before, previous	gawn	ก่อน
be late	maa chaa, maa saai	มาช้า,มาสาย
constant, permanent	talawt welaa	ตลอดเวลา
ever	khoei	เคย
in, still	eek	อีก
in this moment	kamlang	กำลัง
in time	than welaa	ทันเวลา
just	phoeng, muea kee	เพิ่ง, เมื่อกี้
just now	dio nee, tawn nee	เดี๋ยวนี้, ตอนนี้
last	tee laeo	ที่แล้ว
meeting	nat phop	นัดพบ
nearly, almost	kueap ja'	เกือบจะ

TIME & DATE

next	naa	หน้า
normally	pokatee	ปกติ
on time	trong welaa	ตรงเวลา
since	tangtae	ตั้งแต่
sometimes	baang khrang	บางครั้ง
soon	reo reo nee	เร็วๆนี้
urgent	reep	รีบ
waste of time	sia welaa	เสียเวลา

Examples: time

Sorry for being late !

Khaw thoht tee maa chaa !
ขอโทษที่มาช้า

Sorry for let you waiting !

Khaw thoht tee tham hai khun raw !
ขอโทษที่ทำให้คุณรอ

Sorry for disturbing you !

Khaw thoht tee rop kuan khun !

ขอโทษที่รบกวนคุณ

Sorry, but I am busy !

Khaw thoht phom mee thura' !

ขอโทษผมมีธุระ

You should come here on time !

Khun khuan ja' maa theenee trong welaa !

คุณควรจะมาที่นี่ตรงเวลา

How long more ?

Mee welaa eek thaorai ?

มีเวลาอีกเท่าไหร่

Time is up !   Time to go.

Mot welaa !   Daai welaa laeo.

หมดเวลา   ได้เวลาแล้ว

I have to adjust my watch.

Phom tang welaa.

ผมตั้งเวลา

My watch is 3 minutes fast.

Naalikaa phom reo pai saam naathee.

นาฬิกาผมเร็วไปสามนาที

My watch is 3 minutes late.

Naalikaa phom chaa pai saam naathee.

นาฬิกาผมช้าไปสามนาที

My watch goes exactly.

Naalikaa phom trong welaa.

นาฬิกาผมตรงเวลา

My watch stopped working.

Naalikaa taai.

นาฬิกาตาย

Do you have time ?

Do you have time ?

Waang mai ? Mee welaa mai ?
ว่างไหม, มีเวลาไหม

About when ?

Tawn nai ? Pra'maan kee mohng ?
ตอนไหน, ประมาณกี่โมง

Is that too early ?

Reo koen pai rue plao ?
เร็วเกินไปหรือเปล่า

When is it okay ?

Khun saduak mue-arai ?
คุณสะดวกเมื่อไหร่

Whenever.

Mue-rai ko dai.
เมื่อไหร่ก็ได้

Always.

Talawt welaa.
ตลอดเวลา

67

You say when it's best.

Khun waang mue-arai bawk phom.

คุณว่างเมื่อไหร่บอกผม

I have no time.

Mai waang. Kamlang yung.

ไม่ว่างกำลังยุ่ง

That's a bad day for me.

Wan nan mai waang.

วันนั้นไม่ว่าง

This day is okay.

Wan nan ko dai.

วันนั้นก็ได้

Come later.

Dio maa.

เดี๋ยวมา

Come again.

Maa eek na'.

มาอีกนะ

68

SHOPPING

'**sai suea**' = *put on (clothes)* ใส่เสื้อ
'**tot suea**' = *take off (clothes)* ถอดเสื้อ
'**taeng tua**' = *dress nicely* แต่งตัว

clothes	suea phaa	เสื้อผ้า
belt	khemkat	เข็มขัด
blouse	suea	เสื้อ
dress	chut	ชุด
gloves	thung mue	ถุงมือ
hat, cap	muak	หมวก
jacket	suea jacket	เสื้อแจ็กเก็ท
pyjamas	chut nawn	ชุดนอน
sandal	rawng thao tae'	รองเท้าแตะ
shirt	suea	เสื้อ
shoe	rawng thao	รองเท้า
skirt	kra'prohng	กระโปรง
sock	thung thao	ถุงเท้า

suit	suut	สูท
sweater	suea naao	เสื้อหนาว
towel	phaa chet tua	ผ้าเช็ดตัว
trouser	kaang keng	กางเกง
T-shirt	suea yuet	เสื้อยืด

A d d i t i o n a l   w o r d s

bag	kra'pao	กระเป๋า
cotton	phaa faai	ผ้าฝ้าย
hand-made	tham duai mue	ทำด้วยมือ
leather	nang sat	หนังสัตว์
made from...	tham duai	ทำด้วย
market	talaat	ตลาด
present	khawng khwaan	ของขวัญ
quality	khunaphaap	คุณภาพ
sale	lot raakhaa	ลดราคา
silk	phaa mai	ผ้าไหม
special offer	lot phiset	ลดพิเศษ
tailor	raan tat suea	ร้านตัดเสื้อ
type, sort, kind	chanit	ชนิด

Toilet   articles

English	Thai (transliteration)	Thai
brush	praeng	แปรง
comb	wee	หวี
hair shampoo	yaa sa' phom	ยาสระผม
lipstick	lipsatik	ลิปสติก
make - up	khrueang sam aang	เครื่องสำอาง
nail scissors	kankrai tat lep	กรรไกรตัดเล็บ
perfume	nam hawm	น้ำหอม
powder	paeng	แป้ง
razor, shaver	meet kohn	มีดโกน
shaving creme	kreem kohn nuat	ครีมโกนหนวด
soap	sabuu	สบู่
toothbrush	praeng see fan	แปรงสีฟัน
toothpaste	yaa see fan	ยาสีฟัน

'praeng fan' = *brush one's teeth* แปรงฟัน
'kohn nuat' = *shave*   โกนหนวด

73

Colours

English	Phonetic	Thai
colour	see	สี
black	dam	ดำ
brown	namtaan	น้ำตาล
dark blue	nam ngoen	น้ำเงิน
dark brown	namtaan khem	น้ำตาลเข้ม
dark green	khio kae	เขียวแก่
gold	thawng	ทอง
grey	thao	เทา
light blue	faa	ฟ้า
light green	khio awn	เขียวอ่อน
orange	som	ส้ม
pink	chomphuu	ชมพู
red	daeng	แดง
silver	ngoen	เงิน
violet	muang	ม่วง
white	khaao	ขาว
yellow	lueang	เหลือง

Comparison

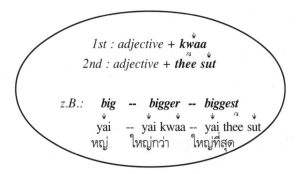

1st : adjective + **kwaa**
2nd : adjective + **thee sut**

z.B.:   **big** -- **bigger** -- **biggest**
         yai -- yai kwaa -- yai thee sut
         หญ่   ใหญ่กว่า   ใหญ่ที่สุด

I go shopping.

Phom/chan pai sue khong.
ผม/ฉันไปซื้อของ

How much is it ?

Raakhaa thaorai ?
ราคาเท่าไหร่

75

That's a little bit too expensive !

Phaeng pai noi !
แพงไปหน่อย

That's too expensive !

Phaeng koen pai !
แพงเกินไป

Can you reduce the price ?

Lot (raakhaa) dai mai ?
ลด(ราคา)ได้ไหม

Do you have something cheaper ?

Thuuk kwaa nee mee mai ?
ถูกกว่านี้มีไหม

Do you have it in a different colour ?

Mee see uen eek mai ?
มีสีอื่นอีกไหม

Can I try it on ?

Khaw lawng sai dai mai ?

ขอลองใส่ได้ไหม

That's too big - too small /
too long - too short / too wide - too tight.

Nee yai-lek / yaao-san / luam-khap koen pai.

นี่ใหญ่-เล็ก / ยาว-สั้น / หลวม-คับ เกินไป

Do you have a bigger size ?

Khun mee thee yai kwaa nee mai khrap/kha ?

คุณมีที่ใหญ่กว่านี้ไหมครับ/ค่ะ

LIVING

House and apartment

> *châo bâan* = rent a house เช่าบ้าน
> *châo hǎwng* = rent a room เช่าห้อง
> *khâa châo* = the rent ค่าเช่า

carpet	phrom	พรม
door	pra'tuu	ประตู
elevator	lif	ลิฟ
entrance	thaang khâo	ทางเข้า
exit	thaang awk	ทางออก
fence	ruua	รั้ว
floor	phuen	พื้น
garden	suan	สวน
house	baan	บ้าน
library	hawng samut	ห้องสมุด
stairs, ladder	bandai	บันได
storey, floor	chan	ชั้น
swimming pool	sa' waai nam	สระว่ายน้ำ
wall	phanang	ผนัง
window	naa taang	หน้าต่าง

L i v i n g   r o o m

hǎwng nǎng lên = *living room* ห้องนั่งเล่น

bookshelf	chán waang nangsue	ชั้นวางหนังสือ
chair	kao-ee	เก้าอี้
radio	withayu'	วิทยุ
sofa	sofa	โซฟา
table	to'	โต๊ะ
telephone	thohrasap	โทรศัพท์
television	thohratat	โทรทัศน์

B a t h r o o m

hǎwng nam = *bathroom* ห้องน้ำ

bathtub	aang aap nam	อ่างอาบน้ำ
mirror	kra'jok	กระจก
toilet	chakrohk	ชักโครก
washbasin	aang laang naa	อ่างล้างหน้า
water tap	kawk nam	ก็อกน้ำ

Kitchen

---

hǎwng khrua = *kitchen* ห้องครัว

---

bottle opener	thee poet khuat	ที่เปิดขวด
cooking pot	maw	หม้อ
fridge	tuu yen	ตู้เย็น
frying pan	kra' tha'	กระทะ
garbage bin	thang khaya'	ถังขยะ
kitchen cupboard	chan waang jaan	ชั้นวางจาน
microwave oven	microwave	ไมโครเวฟ
sink	aang laang jaan	อ่างล้างจาน
stove, oven	tao op	เตาอบ
stove (electric)	tao fai faa	เตาไฟฟ้า
stove (gas)	tao gas	เตาแก๊ส
thermos flask	kratik nam rawn	กระติกน้ำร้อน

LIVING

B e d r o o m

$\widetilde{h}awng\ nawn$ = bedroom ห้องนอน

bed	tiang nawn	เตียงนอน
blanket	phaa hom	ผ้าห่ม
coat hanger	mai khwaen suea	ไม้แขวนเสื้อ
drawer	lin chak	ลิ้นชัก
lamp	khohm fai	โคมไฟ
make-up table	to' khrueang paeng	โต๊ะเครื่องแป้ง
mattress	thee nawn	ที่นอน
pillow	mawn	หมอน
wardrobe, closet	tuu suea phaa	ตู้เสื้อผ้า

WORKING

Occupation --- Job

What do you work ?

Khun tham ngaan arai khrap ?

คุณทำงานอะไรครับ

Where do you work ?

Khun tham ngaan theenai khrap ?

คุณทำงานที่ไหนครับ

What is your profession ?

Khun mee aacheep arai khrap ?

คุณมีอาชีพอะไรครับ

profession	aacheep	อาชีพ
hobby	ngaan adeerek	งานอดิเรก
employee	phanak ngaan	พนักงาน
worker	khon ngaan	คนงาน

cook (man)	phaw khrua	พ่อครัว
cook (woman)	mae khrua	แม่ครัว
dentist	maw fan	หมอฟัน
doctor	maw, phaet	หมอ, แพทย์
electrician	chaang fai faa	ช่างไฟฟ้า
engineer	witsawakon	วิศวกร
farmer	chaao naa	ชาวนา
fisherman	chaao pra'mong	ชาวประมง
hairdresser	chaang tham phom	ช่างทำผม
lawyer	thanaai kwaam	ทนายความ
maid	khon rap chai	คนรับใช้
mechanic	chaang kon	ช่างกล
musician	nak dontree	นักดนตรี
nurse	phayaabaan	พยาบาล
painter	chaang thaa see	ช่างทาสี
photographer	chaang phaap	ช่างภาพ
pilot	nak bin	นักบิน
policeman	tamruat	ตำรวจ
postman	bu rut praisanee	บุรุษไปรษณีย์

secretary	le khaa nu kaan	เลขานุการ
soldier	thahaan	ทหาร
teacher	khruu, aajaan	ครู, อาจารย์
tailor	chaang tat suea	ช่างตัดเสื้อ

Business & School

businessman	nak thurakit	นักธุรกิจ
company	borisat	บริษัท
factory	rohng ngaan	โรงงาน
manager	phuu jat kaan	ผู้จัดการ
owner	jao khawng	เจ้าของ
shop	raan	ร้าน
school	rohng rian	โรงเรียน
primary school	prathom sueksaa	ประถมศึกษา
secondary school	mathayom sueksaa	มัธยมศึกษา
college, academy	withayaalai	วิทยาลัย
university	mahaawithayaalai	มหาวิทยาลัย
student, pupil	nak rian	นักเรียน
test, exam	sawp	สอบ

FAMILY

F a m i l y

family	khrawp khrua	ครอบครัว
parents	phaw mae	พ่อ, แม่
father	phaw	พ่อ
mother	mae	แม่
wife	phanrayaa	ภรรยา
husband	saamee	สามี
son	luuk chaai	ลูกชาย
daugther	luuk saao	ลูกสาว
grandchild	laan	หลาน
younger brother	**nawng** chaai	น้องชาย
elder brother	**phee** chaai	พี่ชาย
younger sister	nawng saao	น้องสาว
elder sister	phee saao	พี่สาว
siblings	phee nong	พี่, น้อง

You have to distinguish between
younger and elder persons.
'nawng' *(younger person)* น้อง
'phee' *(elder person)* พี่

R e l a t i v e s

You have to distinguish between relatives from your father or mother.

relatives	yaat	ญาติ
grandfather (of father)	paw	ปู่
grandfather (of mother)	taa	ตา
grandmother (of father)	yaa	ย่า
grandmother (of mother)	yaai	ยาย
uncle (=brother from father)	aa, lung	อา, ลุง
uncle (=brother from mother)	naa, lung	น้า, ลุง
aunt (=sister from father)	aa, paa	อา, ป้า
aunt (=sister from mother)	naa, paa	น้า, ป้า
niece	laan saao	หลานสาว
nephew	laan chaai	หลานชาย
father-in-law	phaw taa	พ่อตา
mother-in-law	mae yaai	แม่ยาย
son-in-law	luuk khoei	ลูกเขย
daughter-in-law	luuk sa'phai	ลูกสะใภ้

You are in a hurry ?

All you need to know to keep going.

This little book will help you get by in Thailand !

DOCTOR's OFFICE

---

maw = *doctor* หมอ
maw fan = *dentist* หมอฟัน
phayaabaan = *nurse* พยาบาล
rawng phayaabaan = *hospital* โรงพยาบาล

You should see a doctor.

Khit waa khun khuan pai haa maw.
คิดว่าคุณควรไปหาหมอ

I don't feel very well.

Ruusuek mai sabaai. Phom mai sabaai.
รู้สึกไม่สบาย, ผมไม่สบาย

I am feeling (getting) sick.

Ruusuek yaak aajian.
รู้สึกอยากอาเจียน

I feel dizzy.

Ruusuek wian hua.
รู้สึกเวียนหัว

I feel very weak (faintness).

Ruusuek ja' pen lom.
รู้สึกจะเป็นลม

Where does it hurt ?

Jep thee nai ?
เจ็บที่ไหน

It hurts here.

Jep trong nee.
เจ็บตรงนี้

Take three pills (twice) daily.

Kin yaa saam met wan la' khrang (sawng khrang).
กินยาสามเม็ดวันละครั้ง(สองครั้ง)

Help ! = chuai duai !   ช่วยด้วย

Body

English	Transliteration	Thai
body	raang kaai, tua	ร่างกาย, ตัว
ankle	khaw thao	ข้อเท้า
arm	khaen	แขน
back	lang	หลัง
beard	khrao	เครา
blood	lueat	เลือด
bone	kra'duuk	กระดูก
bottom, buttocks	kon	ก้น
brain	samawng	สมอง
breast	nom	นม
cheek	kaem	แก้ม
chest, breast	naaok	หน้าอก
chin	khaang	คาง
ear	huu	หู
elbow	khaw sawgh	ข้อศอก
eye	taa	ตา
eyebrow	khiw	คิ้ว
face	naa	หน้า

95

DOCTOR'S OFFICE

English	Phonetic	Thai
finger	niw	นิ้ว
fingernail	lep mue	เล็บมือ
foot	thao	เท้า
forehead	naa phaak	หน้าผาก
genitals	awaiyawa' phet	อวัยวะเพศ
hair	phom	ผม
hand	mue	มือ
head	hua	หัว
heart	hua chai	หัวใจ
hip	sa' phohk	สะโพก
knee	hua khao	หัวเข่า
leg	khaa	ขา
lip	rim fee paak	ริมฝีปาก
liver	tap	ตับ
lung	pawt	ปอด
mouth	paak	ปาก
muscle	klaam, klaam nuea	กล้าม, กล้ามเนื้อ
mustache	nuat	หนวด
neck	lam khaw	ลำคอ
nerve	sen pra'saat	เส้นประสาท

nose	jamuuk	จมูก
shoulder	baa, lai, baa lai	บ่า, ไหล่, บ่าไหล่
skin	phiw, phiw nang	ผิว, ผิวหนัง
sole	faa thao	ฝ่าเท้า
stomach	thawng	ท้อง
sweat	nguea	เหงื่อ
toenail	lep thao	เล็บเท้า
tongue	lin	ลิ้น
tooth	fan	ฟัน
waist	eo	เอว
wrist	khaw mue	ข้อมือ

Illness

disease, illness	pen rohk	เป็นโรค
burn	mee phlae mai	มีแผลไหม้
cold	pen wat	เป็นหวัด
cough	ai	ไอ
diarrhoea	thawng sia	ท้องเสีย

faint, unconscious	pen lom	เป็นลม
fever	mee khai	มีไข้
flu, influenza	khai wat yai	ไข้หวัดใหญ่
fracture	hak	หัก
hurt	jep, puat	เจ็บ, ปวด
ill, sick	puai, mai sabaai	ป่วย, ไม่สบาย
infection	tit chuea	ติดเชื้อ
insect bite	dohn malaeng kat	โดนแมลงกัด
injury	baat jep	บาดเจ็บ
pain	puat	ปวด
sore throat	jep khaw	เจ็บคอ
sprain	khlet	เคล็ด
sunburn	taet phao	แดดเผา
vomit	aajian	อาเจียน
wound	baat phlae	บาดแผล

Medical Treatment

aspirin	aesphairin	แอสไพริน
bandage	phaa phan phlae	ผ้าพันแผล
diat	lot aahaan	ลดอาหาร
examine	truat	ตรวจ
exercise	awk gam lang kaai	ออกกำลังกาย
health	sukhaphaap	สุขภาพ
injection	cheet yaa	ฉีดยา
medical treatment	raksaa, duu lae	รักษา, ดูแล
medicine	yaa	ยา
painkiller	yaa kae puat	ยาแก้ปวด
pill, tablet	yaa met	ยาเม็ด
plaster	phalastoe	พลาสเตอร์
prescription	bai sang yaa	ใบสั่งยา
sleeping pill	yaa nawn lap	ยานอนหลับ

POST OFFICE & BANK

Important words

account	banchee	บัญชี
airmail	praisanee aakaat	ไปรษณีย์อากาศ
bank	thanaakhaan	ธนาคาร
check	chek	เช็ค
envelope	sawng jotmaai	ซองจดหมาย
express	duan	ด่วน
interest	dawk bia	ดอกเบี้ย
letter	jotmaai	จดหมาย
letterbox, mailbox	tuu praisanee	ตู้ไปรษณีย์
money	ngoen	เงิน
parcel, box	haw, haw khawng	ห่อ, ห่อของ
stamp	sataem	แสตมป์
post card	praisanee yabat	ไปรษณียบัตร
post office	praisanee	ไปรษณีย์
receipt	bai set	ใบเสร็จ
telegram	thohralek	โทรเลข
traveler's check	chek doenthaang	เช็คเดินทาง

receive a letter	rap jotmaai	รับจดหมาย
register a letter	long tha'bian	ลงทะเบียน
send a letter	song jotmaai	ส่งจดหมาย
type a letter	phim jotmaai	พิมพ์จดหมาย
borrow money	khaw yuem ngoen	ขอยืมเงิน
change money	laek ngoen	แลกเงิน
deposit money	faak ngoen	ฝากเงิน
earn money	haa ngoen	หาเงิน
lend money	hai yuem ngoen	ให้ยืมเงิน
save money	kep ngoen	เก็บเงิน
spend money	chai ngoen, sia ngoen	ใช้เงิน, เสียเงิน
waste money	sia daai ngoen	เสียดายเงิน
withdraw money	thawn ngoen	ถอนเงิน
be in debt	pen nee	เป็นหนี้
economical	pra'yat ngoen	ประหยัดเงิน

Examples : Post Office & Bank

Where is the nearest post office ?

Praisanee thee klai theesut yuu theenai khrap/kha' ?
ไปรษณีย์ที่ใกล้ที่สุดอยู่ที่ไหนครับ/ค่ะ

What time is the bank open ?

Thanaakaan poet kee mawng khrap/kha ?
ธนาคารเปิดกี่โมงครับ/ค่ะ

Can I change traveler's checks here?

Khuen chek doenthaang thee nee dai mai ?
ขึ้นเช็คเดินทางที่นี่ได้ไหม

Can I see your passport ?

Khaw duu nangsue doenthaang noi dai mai ?
ขอดูหนังสือเดินทางหน่อยได้ไหม

Can you give me some small change?

Laek ngoen noi dai mai ?
แลกเงินหน่อยได้ไหม

Please change to ....

Khaw laek ngoen pen ngoen.....
ขอแลกเงินเป็นเงิน....

How long does mail take to Europe?

Song jotmaai pai europe chai welaa thaorai ?
ส่งจดหมายไปยุโรปใช้เวลาเท่าไหร่

How much is a letter to Europe?

Song jotmaai pai europe raakhaa thaorai ?
ส่งจดหมายไปยุโรปราคาเท่าไหร่

You are in a hurry ?

All you need to know to keep going.

This little book will help you get by in Thailand !

TELEPHONE

> **thoh** = *to phone*   โทร
> **thoh pai** = *phone somebody*   โทรไป
> **thoh maa** = *phone from somewhere*   โทรมา
> **thoh klap** = *phone back*   โทรกลับ
> **toh saai** = *connect*   ต่อสาย

mobile phone, handy	thohrasap mue tue	โทรศัพท์มือถือ
telephone	thohrasap	โทรศัพท์
telephone bill	khaa thohrasap	ค่าโทรศัพท์
telephone book	samut thohrasap	สมุดโทรศัพท์
telephone box	tuu thohrasap	ตู้โทรศัพท์
telephone number	boe thohrasap	เบอร์โทรศัพท์
answer the phone	rap thohrasap	รับโทรศัพท์
phone somebody	thohrasap, thoh	โทรศัพท์, โทร

overseas call	thohrasap taang pra'thet
	โทรศัพท์ต่างประเทศ
collect call	thohrasap kep ngoen plaai thaang
	โทรศัพท์เก็บเงินปลายทาง
operator	panak ngaan rap thohrasap
	พนักงานรับโทรศัพท์

Who is speaking ?

Khrai phûut khráp ?
ใครพูดครับ

I dialed a wrong number.

Phŏm thoh phìt.
ผมโทรผิด

The line is busy.

Sǎai mâi wâang.
สายไม่ว่าง

Nobody answers.

Mâi mee khrai ráp sǎai.
ไม่มีใครรับสาย

One moment, please.

Raw sàk khrûu khráp/khâ.
Khoi dio khráp/khâ'.
รอสักครู่ครับ/ค่ะ. คอยเดี๋ยวครับ/ค่ะ

That would be everything.

Khâe née ná' khráp/khâ'.
แค่นี้นะครับ/ค่ะ

Can I make an overseas call from here ?

Ja' thohrasap pai taang pra'thet jaak theenee dai mai ?

จะโทรศัพท์ไปต่างประเทศจากที่นี่ได้ไหม

Do you have a telephone listing ?

Mee samut thohrasap mai ?

มีสมุดโทรศัพท์ไหม

With whom would you like to speak ?

Tawng kaan phuut kap khrai khrap ?

ต้องการพูดกลับใครครับ

Would you like to leave a message ?

Mee arai ja' sang mai ?

มีอะไรจะสั่งไหม

Please leave following message:

Karu'naa faak khaw khwaam duai na khrap/kha' :

กรุณาฝากข้อความด้วยนะครับ/ค่ะ

NATURE

Animals --- Plants

animal	sat	สัตว์
flower	dawk mai	ดอกไม้
grass	yaa	หญ้า
orchid	kluai mai	กล้วยไม้
palm tree	ton paam	ต้นปาล์ม
tree	ton mai	ต้นไม้
zoo	suan sat	สวนสัตว์
ant	mot	มด
bird	nok	นก
butterfly	phee suea	ผีเสื้อ
cat	maeo	แมว
chicken	kai	ไก่
cockroach	malaeng saap	แมลงสาบ
cow	wua	วัว
crocodile	jora'khe	จระเข้
dog	maa	หมา
duck	pet	เป็ด

111

elephant	cháang	ช้าง
fish	plaa	ปลา
fly	malaeng wan	แมลงวัน
frog	kòp	กบ
horse	máa	ม้า
kangaroo	jingjôh	จิงโจ้
lion	sǐng toh	สิงโต
lizard	jîng jòk	จิ้งจก
monkey	ling	ลิง
mosquito	yung	ยุง
mouse, rat	nǔu	หนู
parrot	nók gâeo	นกแก้ว
pig	mǔu	หมู
rabbit	kra'tàai	กระต่าย
snake	ngûu	งู
spider	maeng mum	แมงมุม
tiger	sǔea	เสือ
turtle	tào	เต่า

> **'lom'** = *wind* ลม
> **'lom awn awn'** = *breeze* ลมอ่อนๆ
> **'lom chooi'** = *breeze* ลมโชย
> **'lom phat'** = *windy* ลมพัด
> **'lom phat raeng'** = *very windy* ลมพัดแรง

air	aakaat	อากาศ
bay	aao	อ่าว
beach	chaai haat	ชายหาด
cape	laem	แหลม
channel, canal	khlawng	คลอง
cloud	mek	เมฆ
coast	chaai tha'le	ชายทะเล
field	rai naa	ไร่นา
fire	fai	ไฟ
island	ko'	เกาะ
jungle	paa thuep	ป่าทึบ
lake	tha'le saap	ทะเลสาป
moon	pra' jan	พระจันทร์
mountain	phuukhao	ภูเขา

113

NATURE

river	mâe nam	แม่น้ำ
sand	saai	ทราย
sea	thá'le	ทะเล
sky	fáa	ฟ้า
star	daao	ดาว
stone	hin	หิน
sun	phra' aathit	พระอาทิตย์
sunrise	phra' aathit khuen	พระอาทิตย์ขึ้น
sunset	phra' aathit tok	พระอาทิตย์ตก
waterfall	nam tok	น้ำตก
weather	aakaat	อากาศ
wood, forest	paa	ป่า

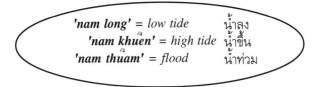

'nam long' = *low tide*   น้ำลง
'nam khuen' = *high tide*   น้ำขึ้น
'nam thuam' = *flood*   น้ำท่วม

Do you play golf ?

TRAVEL

aircondition	khrueang aer	เครื่องแอร์
airplane	khrueang bin	เครื่องบิน
airport	sanaam bin	สนามบิน
arrival	thueng	ถึง
bicycle	rot jakrayaan	รถจักรยาน
bus (regular)	rot thammadaa	รถธรรมดา
bus (with aircondition)	rot prap aakaat	รถปรับอากาศ
bus station	sathaanee rot bas	สถานีรถบัส
bus stop	paai rot me	ป้ายรถเมล์
car	rot	รถ
crash helmet	muak kun nawk	หมวกกันน็อค
departure	awk	ออก
document	ekasaan	เอกสาร
ferry	ruea khaam faak	เรือข้ามฝาก
hotel	rong raem	โรงแรม
motorbike	rot jakrayaan yon	รถจักรยานยนต์
railway	rot fai	รถไฟ
railway station	sathaanee rot fai	สถานีรถไฟ
seaport, harbour	thaa ruea	ท่าเรือ
ship	ruea	เรือ

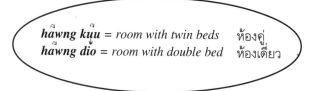

hǎwng kûu = room with twin beds ห้องคู่
hǎwng dio = room with double bed ห้องเดียว

Examples: Traveling

Do you have rooms vacant ?

Mee hǎwng wâang mǎi ?
มีห้องว่างไหม

How much is the night ?

Khâa hǎwng wan lá' thâorai ?
ค่าห้องวันละเท่าไหร่

How long will you stay ?

Khun jǎ' yùu naan thâorai ?
คุณจะอยู่นานเท่าไหร่

118

I don't know yet how long.

Mai saap waa ja' yuu naan thaorai.

ไม่ทราบว่าจะอยู่นานเท่าไหร่

Can I see the room ?

Khaw duu hawng kawn dai mai ?

ขอดูห้องก่อนได้ไหม

Could you bring my luggage please?

Chuai yok kra'pao maa hai noi dai mai ?

ช่วยยกกระเป๋ามาให้หน่อยได้ไหม

Can I put something into the safe ?

Khaw faak khong wai nai tuu sef dai mai ?

ขอฝากของไว้ในตู้เซฟได้ไหม

Can I order food to the room ?

Sang aahaan maa thaan bon hawng dai mai ?

สั่งอาหารมาทานบนห้องได้ไหม

My room number is...

Phom yuu hawng boe ...

ผมอยู่ห้องเบอร์...

I will depart tomorrow.

Phom ja' pai phrung nee.

ผมจะไปพรุ่งนี้

Traveling by car

> *tem tang* = *fill up*   เต็มถัง
> *khrueng tang* = *half full* ครึ่งถัง

accident	ubati het	อุบัติเหตุ
break down	sia	เสีย
car	rot	รถ
car park	thee jawt rot	ที่จอดรถ
car rental charge	khaa chao rot	ค่าเช่ารถ
detour	thaang awm	ทางอ้อม
drive	wing	วิ่ง
drive, steer	khap	ขับ

driving licence	bai khap khee	ใบขับขี่
garage	rhong kep rot	โรงเก็บรถ
insurance	pra'kan	ประกัน
intersection, junction	see yaek	สี่แยก
park	jawt rot	จอดรถ
petrol station	pam nam man	ปั๊มน้ำมัน
refuel	toem nam man	เติมน้ำมัน
short cut	thaang lat	ทางลัด
stop	jawt rot	จอดรถ
take a ride	nang rot len	นั่งรถเล่น
take over	saeng	แซง
tow off	laak rot	ลากรถ
traffic	ja raa jon	จราจร
traffic jam	rot tit	รถติด
traffic lights	fai ja raa jon	ไฟจราจร
turn	liao	เลี้ยว
turn around	klap rot	กลับรถ

Please check the tyre pressure !

Chek lom yaang hai duai !

เช็คลมยางให้ด้วย

Can you repair the car here ?

Theenee sawm rot dai mai ?

ที่นี่ซ่อมรถได้ไหม

How long will it take to repair the car ?

Chai welaa sawm naan pra'maan thaorai ?

ใช้เวลาซ่อมนานประมาณเท่าไหร่

Where can I park the car ?

Jawt dai theenai ?

จอดได้ที่ไหน

I would like to rent a car.

Phom tawnkaan chao rot.

ผมต้องการเช่ารถ

Traveling by train

English	Transliteration	Thai
express train	rot duan	รถด่วน
fast train	rot reo	รถเร็ว
first class	chan nueng	ชั้นหนึ่ง
left-luggage office	thee faak kra'pao	ที่ฝากกระเป๋า
platform	chaan cha laa	ชานชลา
railway	rot fai	รถไฟ
railway station	sathaanee rot fai	สถานีรถไฟ
reservation	jawng tua	จองตั๋ว
return ticket	tua pai klap	ตั๋วไปกลับ
sleeping car	rot nawn	รถนอน
ticket	tua	ตั๋ว
ticket office	chawng khaai tua	ช่องขายตั๋ว
timetable	taa raang rot fai	ตารางรถไฟ

Train to Chiang Mai leaves at 15:00 from platform 1.

Rot fai pai Chiang Mai ja awk chaan cha laa thee 1 welaa baai 3 mohng.

รถไฟไปเชียงใหม่จะออกชานชลาที่ ๑ เวลาบ่าย ๓ โมง

123

City and Country

thit nuea = *north*	ทิศเหนือ
thit tai = *south*	ทิศใต้
thit ta'wan tok = *west*	ทิศตะวันตก
thit ta'wan awk = *east*	ทิศตะวันออก

abroad	taang pra'thet	ต่างประเทศ
address	thee yuu	ที่อยู่
capital city	mueang luang	เมืองหลวง
city, town	mueang	เมือง
country	pra'thet	ประเทศ
district	amphoe	อำเภอ
lane	soi	ซอย
precinct	tambon	ตำบล
province	jangwat	จังหวัด
street	thanon	ถนน
village	muu baan	หมู่บ้าน
world	lohk	โลก
Europe	yurohp	ยุโรป
Thailand	thai	ไทย

TRAVEL

Australia	awsatrelia	ออสเตรเลีย
England	angkrit	อังกฤษ
USA	saharat amerika	สหรัฐอเมริกา
Cambodia	khamaen	เขมร
Laos	laao	ลาว
Malaysia	maalesia	มาเลเซีย
Myanmar	phamaa	พม่า

Directions

saai = *left*	ซ้าย
khwaa = *right*	ขวา
trong pai = *straight ahead*	ตรงไป

above	khaang bon	ข้างบน
around	rawp	รอบ
around the world	rawp lohk	รอบโลก
behind	daan lang	ด้านหลัง
corner	mum	มุม
here	thee nee	ที่นี่
in front	daan naa	ด้านหน้า

in the middle of	trong klaang	ตรงกลาง
in, at	nai	ใน
inside	khaang nai	ข้างใน
next to, beside	daan khaang	ด้านข้าง
opposite	trong khaam	ตรงข้าม
outside	khaang nawk	ข้างนอก
over there	thee nohn	ที่โน่น
there	thee nan	ที่นั่น
under	khaang laang	ข้างล่าง
up to, as far as	jon thueng	จนถึง

More   examples

Is this the way to Pattaya ?

Nee thanon pai Phathayaa chai mai ?
นี่ถนนไปพัทยาใช่ไหม

Which way to Pattaya ?

Pai Phathayaa pai thaang nai ?
ไปพัทยาไปทางไหน

How long does it take to Pattaya ?

Pai Phathayaa chai welaa naan thaorai ?
ไปพัทยาใช้เวลานานเท่าไหร่

What time does the first (last) bus leave for Chonburi ?

Rot thio raek (sut thaai) pai Chonburee kee mohng ?
รถเที่ยวแรก(สุดท้าย)ไปชลบุรีกี่โมง

What a traffic jam today !

Wan nee rot tit maak chai mai ?
วันนี้รถติดมากใช่ไหม

Is it always like this ?

Pen yang nee thuk wan rue plao ?
เป็นยังงี้ทุกวันหรือเปล่า

You can bet on it.
There is always traffic like this.

Nae nawn. Rot tit yang nee thuk wan.
แน่นอน. รถติดอย่างนี้ทุกวัน

127

I better walk.

Phom khit waa phom doen dee kwaa.
ผมคิดว่าผมเดินดีกว่า

It is too far to walk.

Thaang klai maak.
ทางไกลมาก

Pleasant journey !

Thio hai sanuk na' khrap !
เที่ยวให้สนุกนะครับ

You are in a hurry ?

All you need to know to keep going.

This little book will help you get by in Thailand !

FEELINGS

'Heart' - words

Many words which describe feelings begin or end with the word **'jai'**, which actually means **heart**.

Following some important '**heart**' words with short explanations.

dee jai   ดีใจ   **glad**
You can come back to Thailand after a long time and you will be feeling 'dee jai'. This is used frequently for different occassions, but do not confuse it with 'jai dee'.

jai dam   ใจดำ   **careless, ruthless**
Your friend needs your help, but you do not care. They will say you are 'jai dam'.

jai dee   ใจดี   **nice, pleasant**
You help somebody or you are doing somebody a favour without asking. You will hear the compliment 'jai dee'.

FEELINGS

jai yen   ใจเย็น   **calm, cool**
*You are in a traffic jam on your way to the airport and
miss your plane. However, you are not angry, you stay
cool, have '**jai yen**'.
You will hear this word very often. Should you lose
your temper, you will hear '**jai yen yen**'.*

jai ngaai   ใจง่าย   **easily influenced**
*You are a person who can be easily manipulated, you
do what others say.
You have an easy heart, have '**jai ngaai**'.*

jai noi   ใจน้อย   **sensitive**
*Your heart is hurt easily. You are emotionally hurt very
often.*

jai pam   ใจป้ำ   **generous**
*You are going out with friends. When it's time to pay the
bill, you pay everything. You are '**jai pam**'.*

jai rawn   ใจร้อน   **angry, upset**
*You get upset easily. You have a 'hot heart', you are
'**jai rawn**'. You will hear '**jai yen yen**'.*

jep jai   เจ็บใจ   **hurt (emotionally)**
Your wife finds out that you have a minor wife. Your wife will feel 'jep jai'. Be careful.

jing jai   จริงใจ   **honest**
You are honest to others and say the truth. You don't hide your feelings
You have an' honest heart' , you are 'jing jai'.

chuen jai   ชื่นใจ   **pleased**
You are happy, pleased about something or somebody. You are 'chuen jai'.

klum jai   กลุ้มใจ   **concerned, worried**
Your daughter neglects her education and only enjoys her free time. You feel 'klum jai'.

hua jai   หัวใจ   **heart**
This means heart.

khao jai   เข้าใจ   **understand**
You understand what is said or done.

kreng jai   เกรงใจ   **considerate, kind**
You are sitting in a non-smoking taxi. You do not care
about this and smoke. The taxi driver does not say
anything and let you smoke.
He is 'kreng jai'.
This is one of the most important heart words.
Everybody will try to be 'kreng jai'.

mân jai   มั่นใจ   **confident**
You are absolutely sure with your feelings to your
girlfriend. You are 'mân jai'. You also will hear this in
TV spots and advertisements.

nâe jai   แน่ใจ   **sure**
You are sure about something, similar to 'mân jai'.

phuum jai   ภูมิใจ   **proud**
You are proud of something or somebody.
You are 'phuum jai'.

plaeg jai   แปลกใจ   **surprised**
If something surprises you, then you are
'plaeg jai' or also 'pralaat jai'.

prathap jai   ประทับใจ   **impressed**
Thailand impresses you.
You are 'prathap jai' with Thailand.

sabaai jai   สบายใจ   **happy**
You will hear this all the time.
It means happiness and satisfaction.

sao jai   เศร้าใจ   **broken heart, sad**
This means broken heart. You feel sad, have no more
interest in anything; you feel 'sao jai'.

sia jai   เสียใจ   **regret, sorrow, sad**
If you feel sorry for a person, you say 'sia jai'.

son jai   สนใจ   **interested**
You are interested in something or somebody.
You feel 'son jai'.

tang jai   ตั้งใจ   **concentrate**
You are concentrating on what you are doing.
You put all your energy in a project.
You are 'tang jai'.

Additional words

aarom = mood   อารมณ์
aarom dee = be in great mood   อารมณ์ดี
aarom sia = be in bad mood   อารมณ์เสีย
aarom ngut ngit = moody   อารมณ์หงุดหงิด

afraid	klua	กลัว
ambitious, diligent	khayan	ขยัน
angry, furious	kroht, mohhoh	โกรธ, โมโห
annoyed	ramkhaan	รำคาญ
bored	buea	เบื่อ
brave, courageous	klaa haan	กล้าหาญ
cheerful	yindee	ยินดี
confused	sapson	สับสน
cowardly	mai klaa	ไม่กล้า
crazy	baa	บ้า
curious	yaak ruu yaak hen	อยากรู้อยากเห็น
disappointed	phit wang	ผิดหวัง
distrustful	song sai	สงสัย

envious	it chaa	อิจฉา
excited	tuen ten	ตื่นเต้น
false	khee kohng	ขี้โกง
frustrated	kra'won krawaai	กระวนกระวาย
happy	mee khwaam suk	มีความสุข
jealous	hueng	หึง
lazy	khee kiat	ขี้เกียจ
lonely	ngao	เหงา
lovesickness	awk hak	อกหัก
miss	khit thueng	คิดถึง
nervous	ngut ngit	หงุดหงิด
pity	songsaan	สงสาร
playful	khee len	ขี้เล่น
shy	khee aai	ขี้อาย
stingy, mean	khee nio	ขี้เหนียว
worried	kang won	กังวล

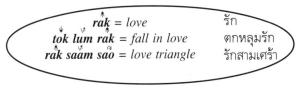

rak = *love* รัก
tok lum rak = *fall in love* ตกหลุมรัก
rak saam sao = *love triangle* รักสามเศร้า

LOVE

G e t   t o   k n o w . . .

Are you here alone ?

Khun maa khon dio rue plao ?
คุณมาคนเดียวหรือเปล่า

Do you like something to drink ?

Khun tawng kaan duem arai mai ?
คุณต้องการดื่มอะไรไหม

May I sit here ?

Nang duai dai mai ?
นั่งด้วยได้ไหม

Somebody sits here already ?

Theenee mee khon nang mai ?
ที่นี่มีคนนั่งไหม

What's your name ?

Khun chue arai ?
คุณชื่ออะไร

Where do you live ?

Baan khun yuu theenai ?

บ้านคุณอยู่ที่ไหน

Where do you come from ?

Khun maa jaak nai ?

คุณมาจากไหน

How old are you ?

Khun aayu' thaorai ?

คุณอายุเท่าไหร่

What do you work ?

Khun tham ngaan arai ?

คุณทำงานอะไร

Where do you work?

Khun tham ngaan theenai?

คุณทำงานที่ไหน

What do you do in your free time ?

Khun tham arai welaa waang ?

คุณทำอะไรเวลาว่าง

Do you come here often ?

Khun maa theenee boi mai ?

คุณมาที่นี่บ่อยไหม

Should we go already ?

Pai kan rǔe yang ?
ไปกันหรือยัง

Let's go !

Pai kan dai laeo !
ไปกันได้แล้ว

I want to stay here longer.

Yaak yuu taw eek noi.
อยากอยู่ต่ออีกหน่อย

I will bring you home.

Phom ja' song khun klap baan.
ผมจะส่งคุณกลับบ้าน

I want to know more about you.

Phom yaak ruu jak khun maak kwaa nee.
ผมอยากรู้จักคุณมากกว่านี้

We think the same, don't we ?

Rao khit muean kan chai mai ?
เราคิดเหมือนกันใช่ไหม

Should we meet again ?

Rao ja' phop kan eek mai ?
เราจะพบกันอีกไหม

When can I meet you again ?

Ja' phop khun eek muearai ?
จะพบคุณอีกเมื่อไหร่

Can I have your telephone number ?

Khaw boe thohrasap khun dai mai ?
ขอเบอร์โทรศัพท์คุณได้ไหม

Can I call you ?

Phom thoh haa khun dai mai ?
ผมโทรหาคุณได้ไหม

See you soon.

Rao phop kan eek.

แล้วพบกันอีก

See you tomorrow.

Phop kan phrung nee.

พบกันพรุ่งนี้

Take care.

Duulae tua eng duai na'.

ดูแลตัวเองด้วยนะ

Love stories

Love makes blind.

Kwaam rak tham hai khon taa bawt.

ความรักทำให้คนตาบอด

I am crazy for you.

Phom/Chan khlang khlai nai tua khun.

ผม/ ฉันคลั่งใคล้ในตัวคุณ

I love you.

Phom/Chan rak khun.

ผม/ฉันรักคุณ

You are beautiful.

Khun suai jang loei.
คุณสวยจังเลย

You are handsome.

Khun law jang loei.
คุณหล่อจังเลย

You are so cute.

Khun naa rak jang loei.
คุณน่ารักจังเลย

*The words **jang loei** will be added here often, but actually don't have a meaning.*

You have beautiful eyes.

Taa khun suai jang loei.
ตาคุณสวยจังเลย

You have a wonderful smile.

Khun yim suai jang loei.
คุณยิ้มสวยจังเลย

144

I want to stay with you.

Phom/Chan yaak yuu kap khun.

ผม/ฉันอยากอยู่กับคุณ

Farewell

Will you send a letter ?

Khun ja' khian jotmaai thueng chan rue plao.

คุณจะเขียนจดหมายถึงผม/ ฉันหรือเปล่า

I will send you a letter.

Phom ja' khian jotmaai thueng khun.

ผม/ ฉันจะเขียนจดหมายถึงคุณ

I will call you from England.

Phom ja' thoh haa khun jaak angkrit.

ผม/ฉันจะโทรหาคุณจากอังกฤษ

I will come back soon.

Phom ja' klap maa reo reo nee.

ผมจะกลับมาเร็วๆนี้

I have to leave because of my job.

Phom tawng klap pai tham ngaan.

ผมต้องกลับไปทำงาน

Wait until I come back.

Raw phom klap maa na'.

รอผมกลับมานะ

Don't forget to write !

Yaa luem khian jotmaai maa baang na' !

อย่าลืมเขียนจดหมายมาบ้างนะ

Don't cry.

Yaa rong hai.

อย่าร้องไห้

Wipe your tears.

Chet nam taa.

เช็ดน้ำตา

I can't take it.

Phom/Chan thon mai dai.
ผม/ฉันทนไม่ได้

I miss you.

Khit thueng khun.
คิดถึงคุณ

I have to think about you all the times.

Phom/Chan khit thueng khun samoe samoe.
ผม/ฉันคิดถึงคุณเสมอๆ

I will always love you.

Ja' rak khun talawt pai.
จะรักคุณตลอดไป

147

Important   PHRASES

What you will hear all the times !

1. mai pen rai   ไม่เป็นไร   **It doesn't matter !**
You will hear this phrase many times. You are in a traffic jam and miss your plane. You are desperate and upset. But you should relax and tell yourself 'mai pen rai'.
Don't think Thais don't care. Don't misunderstand this phrase. Everybody just tries to cope with one's fate and tries to stay calm whatever happens. There is no point to get upset. The plane won't return.

2. jai yen yen   ใจเย็นเย็น   **calm, cool**
This phrase is widely used together with 'mai pen rai'. It means 'cool heart'.
Stay calm and don't get upset or lose your temper. If you get angry, you will hear 'jai yen yen'.

3. sanuk   สนุก   **fun**
Thais love to have fun. They know how to entertain and having a good time.
Thais don't like to sit home alone. They enjoy going out together and having fun.
Even during a financial crisis everybody takes it easy and enjoys life as much as possible.

149

IMPORTANT PHRASES

We are sure you will have lots of fun in Thailand and won't get bored.

4. sabaai สบาย **happy**

You will get asked 'sabaai mai?' many times. 'Sabaai' means happy and satisfied and 'mai' is the particle to form a question. You will most probable answer 'sabaai maak'.

5. double words

Sometimes you will hear some words repeated. This is done to emphasis. Words, which are widely used, are for example 'maak-maak' (very much), 'jing - jing' (100% sure), 'reo – reo' (very fast), 'chaa – chaa' (very slow) or also 'jai yen yen' (cool heart).

6. nicknames

Most Thai people use nicknames instead of their real names. You will be surprised about some translations of these nicknames. These nicknames have meanings like 'rat', 'pig', 'sugar' or even 'Pepsi' like our Thai editor. But don't forget to use the particle 'Khun' (= Mr., Mrs., Miss) with these nicknames.

If your nickname will be 'Fatty', don't get angry.

7. rue plao, laeo rue yang   หรือเปล่า, แล้วหรือยัง
*Some questions end with **'rue plao'** or with **'laeo rue yang'**. This has the meaning of 'or not ?' and 'already or not yet?'.*

8. chai mai   ใช่ไหม
*Other questions end with **'chai mai'**. This can be translated with 'is it, isn't it'. (see also chapter question & answer, pages 44-51)*

9. dai mai   ได้ไหม
*Many questions end with **'dai mai'**. 'dai' means 'to be able, can' and **'mai'** is the particle to form a question.*

10. riap roi   เรียบร้อย   ready, okay
*The question **'riap roi laeo ?'** means' **Is everything ready, okay ?'**.*

151

RESTAURANT and BAR

raan aahaan = *smaller restaurant*   ร้านอาหาร
phataakaan = *bigger restaurant*   ภัตตาคาร

aahaan = *food*   อาหาร
aahaan chao = *breakfast*   อาหารเช้า
aahaan klang wan = *lunch*   อาหารกลางวัน
aahaan yen = *dinner*   อาหารเย็น
aahaan kham = *late night snack*   อาหารค่ำ

hiw nam = *thirsty*   หิวน้ำ
hiw khaao = *hungry*   หิวข้าว

Important words

English	Phonetic	Thai
ashtray	thee khia bu'ree	ที่เขี่ยบุหรี่
bottle	khuat	ขวด
bottle opener	thee poet khuat	ที่เปิดขวด
bowl	chaam	ชาม
chair	kaoee	เก้าอี้
chopsticks	ta'kiap	ตะเกียบ
cigarettes	bu'ree	บุหรี่
cup	thuay	ถ้วย
drink	duem	ดื่ม
eat	kin khaao	กินข้าว
food	aahaan	อาหาร
fork	sawm	ช้อม
glass	kaeo	แก้ว
knife	meet	มีด
lighter	fai chaek	ไฟแช็ค
market	talaat	ตลาด
matches	mai kheet fai	ไม้ขีดไฟ
menu	menuu	เมนู

napkin	kradaat	กระดาษ
plate	jaan	จาน
smoking	suup bu'ree	สูบบุหรี่
spoon	chawn	ช้อน
service, waiter	dek soef aahaan	เด็กเสริฟอาหาร
table	to'	โต๊ะ
tablecloth	phaa puu to'	ผ้าปูโต๊ะ
toothpick	mai jim fan	ไม้จิ้มฟัน

Drinks

| water | nam | น้ำ |
| ice cubes | nam khaeng | น้ำแข็ง |

coffee (hot or cold)	kaafae	กาแฟ
coffee (hot, milk & sugar)	kaafae rawn	กาแฟร้อน
iced coffee (milk & sugar)	kaafae yen	กาแฟเย็น
milk	nom	นม

---

mai sai nam taan = without sugar   ไม่ใส่น้ำตาล
ao waan waan = sweet   เอาหวานๆ
ao nom maak maak = with a lot of milk   เอานมมากๆ

155

tea (hot or cold)	chaa	ชา
tea (hot, milk & sugar)	chaa ráwn	ชาร้อน
iced tea (milk & sugar)	chaa yen	ชาเย็น
fruit juices	nám phŏnlamai	น้ำผลไม้

***nám + name of fruit** = fruit juice*
*for example: **nám sàpparót** = pineapple juice*

In Thailand one adds a little bit of salt to
fresh fruit juices. If you would like to have
your fruit juice without any salt, you say:
***mâi sài kluea**.*

ไม่ใส่เกลือ

Fruits

phonlamai = *fruits*   ผลไม้

apple	aeppaen	แอปเปิ้ล
banana	kluai	กล้วย
coconut	ma'praao	มะพร้าว
durian	turian	ทุเรียน
grape	angun	องุ่น
guava	farang	ฝรั่ง
jackfruit	khanun	ขนุน
lime	ma'naao	มะนาว
longan	lamyai	ลำใย
lychee	linchee	ลิ้นจี่
mango	ma'muang	มะม่วง
mangosteen	mangkhut	มังคุด
orange	som	ส้ม
papaya	ma'la'kaw	มะละกอ
pineapple	sapparot	สับปะรด
pomelo	som-oh	ส้มโอ

rambutan	ngo'	เงาะ
roseapple	chomphuu	ชมพู่
sugarapple	noi naa	น้อยหน่า
tamarind	ma'khaam	มะขาม
watermelon	taeng moh	แตงโม

Cooking terms

> **tham kap khaao** = *cook*   ทำกับข้าว

bake	awp	อบ
boil	tom	ต้ม
chopped	sap	สับ
deep fry	thawt	ทอด
fry	phat	ผัด
grill	yaang, phao	ย่าง, เผา
raw	dip	ดิบ
stew, steam	nueng	นึ่ง
toast	ping	ปิ้ง
(well) done	suk	สุก

Taste & Flavour

> **rot** = *flavour* รส
> **chim** = *to taste* ชิม

bitter	khom	ขม
crisp	krawp	กรอบ
salty	khem	เค็ม
sour	prio	เปรี้ยว
spicy, hot	phet	เผ็ด
sweet	waan	หวาน
sweet & sour	prio - waan	เปรี้ยว – หวาน
tasteless	juet	จืด

Spices

fish sauce	nam plaa	น้ำปลา
pepper	phrik thai	พริกไท
salt	kluea	เกลือ
sauce	saws	ซอส
sugar	nam taan	น้ำตาล
vinegar	nam som saai chuu	น้ำส้มสายชู

T h a i   s p i c e s

nam jim   น้ำจิ้ม

sauce -- on nearly every table in all restaurants

nam som phrik dawng   น้ำส้มพริกดอง

vinegar-with chilli

nam plaa   น้ำปลา

fisch sauce -- is used instead of salt

ka'pi'   กะปิ

shrimp paste-- made from very tiny shrimps

nam phrik ka'pi'   น้ำพริกกะปิ

shrimp sauce – spicy

saws phrik   ซอสพริก

chilli sauce -- similar to ketchup, but spicy, with tomatos, garlic and chilli *nâm phrík núm*   น้ำพริกหนุ่ม

chilli sauce -- from Northern Thailand, spicy, green colour

prík phao   พริกเผา

chilli -- chopped and roasted chillies

nâm phrík phǎo   น้ำพริกเผา

chilli paste – from *phrík phao*, garlic, onions and *nam plaa*

phrík pon   พริกป่น

chilli powder

seeiw khǎao / seeiw dam   ซีอิ๊วขาว / ซีอิ๊วดำ

soy sauce -- called black or white soy sauce, but both are black in colour

nâm man hǒi   น้ำมันหอย

oyster sauce -- is used for cooking

Small snacks

kap klaem = *snack*   กับแกล้ม

shrimp chips	khaao kriap kung	ข้าวเกรียบกุ้ง
potato chips	man farang thawt	มันฝรั่งทอด
cashew nuts	met ma'muang thawt	เม็ดมะม่วงทอด
peanuts	thua thawt	ถั่วทอด
fish cake	thawt man plaa	ทอดมันปลา
roasted eggs	khai ping	ไข่ปิ้ง
meat balls	luuk chin ping	ลูกชิ้นปิ้ง
hot dog	sai krawk	ไส้กรอก
spring roll	paw pia' thawt	ปอเปี๊ยะทอด
satay	sa'te'	สะเต๊ะ
spare ribs	see khrohng muu thawt	ซี่โครงหมูทอด

som tam = *papaya salad --
made from green papaya, lemon,
sugar, fish sauce, tomato, garlic, tiny
tried shrimps or crab and lots of
chillies.
Very spicy !*

Breakfast

English	Phonetic	Thai
egg	khái	ไข่
boiled eggs	khái tom	ไข่ต้ม
half boiled eggs	khái luak	ไข่ลวก
plain omelet	khái jio	ไข่เจียว
stuffed omelet	khái yat sai	ไข่ยัดไส้
scrambled eggs	khái khon	ไข่คน
fried eggs	khái daao	ไขดาว่
bread	khanom pang	ขนมปัง
butter	noei	เนย
jam, marmalade	yaem	แยม
honey	nam phueng	น้ำผึ้ง

Salads

yam = Thai salad -- delicious, but very spicy. Is eaten as first course or small snack in the bar.

prawn salad	yam kung	ยำกุ้ง
mixed salad	yam ruam mit	ยำรวมมิตร
glass noodle salad	yam wunsen	ยำวุ้นเส้น
seafood salad	yam ruam mit tha'le	ยำรวมมิตรทะเล
beef salad	yam nuea	ยำเนื้อ
squid salad	yam plaa muek	ยำปลาหมึก
sausage salad	yam sai krawk	ยำไส้กรอก

laap = Thai salad -- cooked and chopped, spicy, from Isaan (North-East Thailand)

duck salad	laap pet	ลาบเป็ด
chicken salad	laap kai	ลาบไก่
beef salad	laap nuea	ลาบเนื้อ
pork salad	laap muu	ลาบหมู

Soups

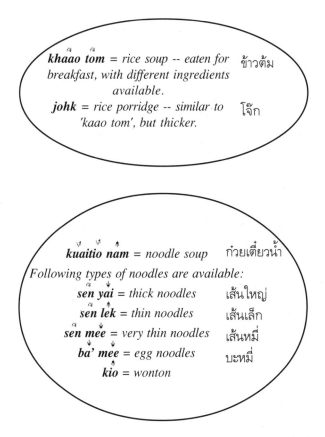

khaao tom = *rice soup -- eaten for breakfast, with different ingredients available.* ข้าวต้ม

johk = *rice porridge -- similar to 'kaao tom', but thicker.* โจ๊ก

kuaitio nam = *noodle soup* ก๋วยเตี๋ยวน้ำ

Following types of noodles are available:

sen yai = *thick noodles* เส้นใหญ่

sen lek = *thin noodles* เส้นเล็ก

sen mee = *very thin noodles* เส้นหมี่

ba' mee = *egg noodles* บะหมี่

kio = *wonton*

> **tom yam** = *spicy - sour - soup*
> *probably the Thai national dish*

tom yam kung   ต้มยำกุ้ง

prawn soup – spicy, with lemon grass

tom yam po' taek, po' taek   ต้มยำโป๊ะแตก, โป๊ะแตก

seafood soup -- with mussels, prawns, crabs, fish, etc.

Other soups

tom khaa kai   ต้มข่าไก่

chicken soup --similar to *'tom yam'*, with coconut milk

tom juet wunsen muu sap   ต้มจืดวุ้นเส้นหมูสับ

vegetable soup -- with chopped & minced pork (= muu sap) and glass noodles

tom som plaa   ต้มส้มปลา

fish soup -- sour & spicy

Curry

kaeng ka'ree kai   แกงกะหรี่ไก่

curry -- with coconut milk and chicken

kaeng khio waan muu   แกงเขียวหวานหมู

curry -- green, sweet-sour curry with pork

kaeng phanaeng nuea   แกงแพนงเนื้อ

curry -- thick curry with coconut milk and beef

kaeng phet kai   แกงเผ็ดไก่

curry – spicy, with red chillies and chicken

haw mok tha'le   ห่อหมกทะเล

seafood curry -- thick, with coconut milk, steamed in banana leaves

Rice dishes

> **khaao** = rice   ข้าว
> **khaao nio** = sticky rice   ข้าวเหนียว

Rice is the main constituent in Thai food and there is an enormous varity of dishes with rice. Most dishes are served with rice and topped with chicken, pork, etc. Following a few typical dishes:

khaao man kai   ข้าวมันไก่

chicken on rice -- thin cut chicken meat on rice with chicken soup

khaao muu daeng   ข้าวหมูแดง

pork on rice -- red pork meat on rice

khaao muu krawp   ข้าวหมูกรอบ

rice and pork -- crispy pork and rice

Pasta

kuaitio haeng   ก๋วยเตี๋ยวแห้ง

noodles without soup (see SOUPS, page 165 for different ingredients)

phat thai   ผัดไทย

fried noodles – *'sen lek'* fried with prawns, vegetable, eggs and peanuts

phat seeiw   ผัดซีอิ๊ว

noodles with soy sauce – *'sen yai'* fried with black soy sauce

khanom jeen nam yaa   ขนมจีนน้ำยา

noodles with fish curry

mee krawp   หมี่กรอบ

crisp noodles -- crispy fried noodles with prawns and bean sprouts

raat naa   ราดหน้า

noodles with thick sauce

169

Seafood

aahǎan tha'le = seafood   อาหารทะเล

fish	plaa	ปลา
perch	plaa ka'phong	ปลากะพง
shark	plaa chalaam	ปลาฉลาม
tuna	plaa oh	ปลาโอ
squid	plaa muek	ปลาหมึก

oyster	hoi naang rom	หอยนางรม
cockle	hoi kraeng	หอยแครง
mussels	hoi malaeng phuu	หอยแมลงภู่
clams	hoi laai	หอยลาย

river crab	kang	กั้ง
crab	puu	ปู
prawn	kung	กุ้ง
lobster	kung mang kon	กุ้งมังกร
tiger prawn	kung kam kaam	กุ้งก้ามกาม

Seafood dishes

plaa prio waan   ปลาเปรี้ยวหวาน

fish -- sweet & sour, with tomatos, pineapple, etc.

plaa thawt   ปลาทอด

fish -- fried fish, dipping sauce

plaa nueng ma'naao   ปลานึ่งมะนาว

fish -- steamed in lime sauce and chillies

plaa nueng pae' sa'   ปลานึ่งแป๊ะซะ

fish -- steamed with mushrooms and coriander

plaa raat phrik   ปลาราดพริก

fish -- fried with chilli dressing

plaa muek yat sai   ปลาหมึกยัดไส้

squid -- filled with minced pork meat

hoi laai phat nam phrik phao   หอยลายผัดน้ำพริกเผา

clams -- fried in chilli sauce

171

hŏi naang rom sòt   หอยนางรมสด

oyster -- on ice, with lime and onions

hŏi malaeng phŭu àwp maw din   หอยแมลงภู่อบหม้อดิน

mussels -- steamed, chilli sauce for dipping

kŭng phăo   กุ้งเผา

prawns -- grilled, chilli sauce for dipping

kŭng chup paeng thâwt   กุ้งชุบแป้งทอด

prawns – fried

kŭng chae nám plaa   กุ้งแช่น้ำปลา

shrimps – raw, with garlic, lime and chilli sauce

kŭng mang kon phàt nám phrík phăo

lobster -- fried with chilli sauce   กุ้งมังกรผัดน้ำพริกเผา

kâam puu nûeng   ก้ามปูนึ่ง

crab -- steamed, chilli sauce for dipping

D i s h e s - quick and easy

khaao phat   ข้าวผัด

fried rice -- with pork, chicken, crab or prawns available

kai phat nawmai   ไก่ผัดหน่อไม้

chicken -- fried with bamboo sprouts

nuea phat nam man hoi   เนื้อผัดน้ำมันหอย

beef -- fried in oyster sauce

muu phat kra'thiam prik thai   หมูผัดกระเทียมพริกไทย

pork -- fried with garlic and pepper

kung phat nam phrik phao   กุ้งผัดน้ำพริกเผา

prawns -- fried in roasted chillies

phat phak ruam mit   ผัดผักรวมมิตร

vegetable -- fried for a short time only

Sweets

khanom = sweets   ขนม

nam khaeng sai   น้ำแข็งใส

sweets -- sugar peas, beans, potatos, sticky rice, fruits, coconut creme, crushed ice

sang khayaa   สังขยา

pudding -- made from pumpkin, eggs, sugar and coconut creme

foi tawng   ฝอยทอง

egg yolk -- fried in sweet syrup

khaao nio ma'muang   ข้าวเหนียวมะม่วง

sticky rice -- served with fresh mangos and coconut creme

khaao laam   ข้าวหลาม

sticky rice -- with coconut creme and black beans in the bamboo stick *khaao tom mat*   ข้าวต้มมัด

sticky rice -- in palm leaves with bananas and black beans

kluai chueam   กล้วยเชื่อม

bananas -- backed in sweet syrup

luuk chup   ลูกชุบ

candy -- beans with jelly glaze

ta' koh   ตะโก้

candy -- in palm leaves with coconut creme

khanom bueang   ขนมเบื้อง

biscuit, cookie -- with egg yolk and coconut creme or salty with onions

saarim   ซาหริ่ม

candy noodles -- with sugar peas, coconut milk and crushed ice

At the restaurant

A table for two, please.

To' samrap sawng khon.
โต๊ะสำหรับสองคน

I am expecting some friends.

Phom kamlang raw phuean.
ผมกำลังรอเพื่อน

Can I see the menu.

Khaw menuu noi khrap.
ขอเมนูหน่อยครับ

I did not order this.

Phom mai dai sang jaan nee.
ผมไม่ได้สั่งจานนี้

Did you order already ?

Sang laeo rue yang khrap ?
สั่งแล้วหรือยังครับ

I did not eat yet.

Phŏm yang mai dai thaan khaao.

ผมยังไม่ได้ทานข้าว

What would you like to eat ?

Khun yaak thaan arai ?

คุณอยากทานอะไร

Would you like to taste ?

Chim noi mai ?

ชิมหน่อยไหม

That looks delicious.

Duu naa thaan.

ดูน่าทาน

That smells delicious.

Hawm naa thaan.

หอมน่าทาน

Delicious ?

Aroi mai ?

อร่อยไหม

Very delicious.

Aroi maak.

อร่อยมาก

Are you still hungry ?

Im laeo rue yang ?

อิ่มแล้วหรือยัง

I am full.

Im laeo.

อิ่มแล้ว

Pay, please ! The bill, please !

Kep ngoen duai ! Chek bin duai !

เก็บเงินด้วย/ เช็คบิลด้วย

In the bar

I am thirsty.

Hiw nam.
หิวน้ำ

What would you like to drink ?

Khun tawng kaan duem arai ?
คุณต้องการดื่มอะไร

I want to drink beer.

Yaak duem bia.
อยากดื่มเบียร์

Cheers!

Chon kaeo !
ชนแก้ว

You can drink !

Duem keng jang.

ดื่มเก่งจัง

How much did you drink already ?

Khun duem kee kaeo laeo ?

คุณดื่มกี่แก้วแล้ว

Are you drunk ?

Mao laeo rue yang ?

เมาแล้วหรือยัง

Didn't you drink a little bit too much ?

Mao maak pai rue plao ?

เมามากไปหรือเปล่า

You better stop drinking now.

Naa ja' yut duem dai laeo.

น่าจะหยุดดื่มได้แล้ว

INDEX

187

INDEX

188